# A Quiver Of Flowers

**Poems by Raghu Tantry**

*Illustrations and Cover Photo by Raghu Tantry*

authorHOUSE®

*AuthorHouse*™
*1663 Liberty Drive, Suite 200*
*Bloomington, IN 47403*
*www.authorhouse.com*
*Phone: 1-800-839-8640*

*© 2009 Raghu Tantry. All rights reserved.*

*No part of this book may be reproduced, stored in a retrieval system, or transmitted by any means without the written permission of the author.*

*First published by AuthorHouse 10/1/2009*

*ISBN: 978-1-4490-1141-3 (e)*
*ISBN: 978-1-4490-1140-6 (sc)*

*Printed in the United States of America*
*Bloomington, Indiana*

*This book is printed on acid-free paper.*

# **Preface**

I started writing poetry when I was in primary school. The first one probably was about the bees that toiled to make honey, while the honey is robbed by humans - with little consideration for the lives of the bees. I am a vegetarian, but I did not stop eating honey or foods that contain honey. Value systems, as I see them, are as complex as the human mind - and are in truth relative to time, culture, and situations.

From that time onwards, I learned that every human has the same God-given spiritual make up, but what each one does with it is based on the individual's interactions and experiences with his family and society, his circumstances and stature in life, and his aspirations. I have been writing poetry since childhood, and most of them were very optimistic and happy. I was trying to find meaning in madness, and joy in everything.

Some of my earlier poems were pessimistic or even cynical, reflecting the strange overwhelming situations I was writing them in. Yet, the process of editing them over days, or over months, or some even over several years, helped me edit my own view of life, and the people I live with. I believe that writing poems as they emerge, and honestly editing them, is actually a therapeutic process.

I realize that no opinion, no view point about a person, place, thing, or life situation is un-editable. Even the Books and Scriptures are editable. We see as a mundane fact, the evolution of the animal kingdom, evolution of the human race, and evolution of the human mind and spirit. Human evolution is essentially a divine process involving the highest level of editing by the Great Editor. Every progressive religion has repeatedly edited its scriptures for the benefit of humanity.

Writing the poems, and reading them later myself, have often provided me deeper understanding of myself and the world around me. I often look at this world as a gathering of spirits seeking ways to be known, to be loved and respected. The businessman, the movie star, the politician, the athlete, the artist, and even the monk are seeking these things. How they handle themselves spiritually will determine how they will be known, loved and respected.

*Raghu Tantry*

# *Review*

The study and appreciation of poetry, seems to have focused on mostly 4 countries and their contributions: American (Emerson, Whitman, Thoreau), English (Byron, Jonson, Milton, Tennyson), French (Villon, Labe, La Fontaine, Cocteau), and Greek (Sappho, Homer, Solon, Semonides).

But there is an entire poetic history that has been largely ignored by us in the West. It is a history with language and imagery that rivals that of ancient Greece in grandeur, or that of the Leaves of Grass in its transcendentalism.

The poetic genius of India is older than most of recorded history. Going back to the days of the Vedic's, the great epic myths of the Hindus can stand against those of Homer, and the works of modern Indian poets such as Tulsidas, Mirabai, Chandidas, and Kabir rivalled anything that the western world has produced in the last 1000 years.

Indeed, these poets were not just revered as great artists and seers, but were elevated to the ranks of saints. Their words were so powerful and beautiful that –surely- they must have been inspired by the Gods.

It is by reminding us of those great works, that A Quiver of Flowers will act as a introduction into that rich eastern history.

Raghunath Tantry (affectionately known as Raghu to his friends) has written what can only be called a great modern re-introduction to the oral history of India. At once, A Quiver of Flowers is a great work of timeless topics, universal in their experiences and appeal, while at the same time infused with the cadence and rhythm of a 6000 year old poetic history of a people.

In pieces such as Potent Boons and Silence, Raghu invites us to share in a rediscovery of an ancient art form while still allowing readers to relate to them on personal and emotional levels. His use of classical Indian imagery and pacing, serves to make the contemporary, exotic, and the familiar new again.

Like all great Indian poetry, Raghu lets poetry give voice to the world around us, anthropomorphising everything from the maple leaves to gravity to the banyan tree.

There is nothing pretentious in Raghu's words, even when he modernizes his style in pieces such as I See Good People or Omnibus. Crisp, direct, yet full of life, A Quiver of Flowers is perfect for those that wish to read –not only with the eyes and mind- but with the heart as well. Beautiful and moving, it is a work that cannot be put down when started.

It is a great work, and an important contribution to the development of and the appreciation for poetry on a universal basis. Indeed, it serves as the first great example of 'flat earth' poetry –but this time, it is the East exporting its values to the West.

This is not just a work that must be bought and read. It is a work that must be shared with all those you love.

***Yusuf Gad***

# *Review*

The Quiver of Flowers does make one experience a flowery quiver. The vast spectrum of topics on which philosophical incising has been done, makes one think whether we are here to just abide by routines, or is there something beyond this in our lives.

Raghu, as I dearly know him for last two decades, is a thorough professional, with a richly gifted and talented mind for abstract thinking. Only being a dedicated poet is definitely great, but a professional indulging in poetry results in a new dimension in writing poems.

Just as his professionalism has taken poems to a new divide, the poetic sense has made Raghu a better professional, who thinks with both mind and heart.

Good work done, Raghu! I envy the new dimensions in your life, and only wonder when I will be able to follow a similar path.

All the best!

*Dr R K Sanghavi*

# *Review*

A Quiver of Flowers weaves poetically through the tapestry of life. Raghu has infused into it all the threads of life, sorrow, pain, gloom, deceit, despair, joy, hope and above all spiritual enlightenment. The result is lyrical poetry at its best – elevated to the realm of Sufism.

Raghu's poems are intertwined with a strong streak of hope that the human race can rise above their differences and live peacefully and happily, and the world does not need to be conquered with a quiver of arrows but with a quiver of flowers.

Reading Raghu's poems was a pleasure. I wish him all the best and every success. Hope this will be the first of many works of poetry that will be published by Raghu.

*Noor Jehan*

# *Review*

As I went through each and every poem, my one thought was - how true. In this age of AK47 and suicide bombing, "A Quiver of Flowers" does pierce the heart only to release the soul within you. Its philosophical bend makes you feel so serene and at peace with yourself. The ones which liked most are Faithful Quilt, Potent Boons, and My Mother Alone.

**Sita Padakannaya**

# *Review*

I read Raghu's poems with great empathy. Raghu's poems are short and sweet, philosophical and thought provoking. I had re-read many of the poems to grasp their inner meaning. My favorite poems are Banyan Trees of Miami, Effort, Faithful Quilt, Wise Quilt, I See Good People, Parallel Lines, Potent Boons and Magic Land. Raghu's poems have the flavors of science, pharmacy and industry/ business.... for instance, detoxified (in Being Human), toxic years (in Colorful Positives), balmy lyrics (in Latent Poem), chemical industry and lucrative contract (in Modern Forgiveness), deadly syndrome (in Potent Boons), heart disease (in Law of Gravity), and fevered brain (in Poems). I liked the poems a lot - keep writing Raghu!

**Satya Adhikary**

# REVIEW

'A Quiver of Flowers', a collection of short poems by Raghu Tantry is a blend of spirituality, honesty, child-like curiosity and life experiences all narrated with impeccable consistency and a simple yet fine tone. The poems such as 'Faithful Quilt' takes readers through a spiritual ride with as mundane a topic as a quilt.

The inspirations for Raghu's poems such as 'Banyan Trees of Miami', 'Faithful Quilt', and 'Omnibus' gives readers a glimpse of Raghu's artistic and creative genius in turning such simple subjects to one which can be reflected on a much higher spiritual level.

Raghu's work serves as an inspiration to any budding poet. Raghu's talent in taking profound disciplines such as philosophy and culture, and turning them into an excellent collection of easy to understand poems is what makes his collection stand apart.

I wish Raghu all the best and continued success in his creative endeavors.

*Avinash Bhaskar*

# Contents

- Preface ..................................................................... iii
- Reviews ...................................................................... v

[1] Banyan Trees Of Miami ................................................ 1

[2] Being Human ............................................................. 5

[3] Child ............................................................................ 9

[4] Colorful Positives ..................................................... 11

[5] Donkey Speaks Out ................................................. 13

[6] Effort ........................................................................ 17

[7] Faithful Quilt ........................................................... 21

[8] Futile Feelings ......................................................... 23

[9] Gain and Pain .......................................................... 25

[10] I See Good People ................................................. 27

[11] Labor ..................................................................... 31

[12] Latent Poem .......................................................... 33

[13] Law Of Gravity ..................................................... 35

[14] Living Alone Is Fun .............................................. 39

[15] Magic Land ........................................................... 41

[16] Maiden Rose ......................................................... 45

[17] Mania ................................................................... 47

[18] Maple Celebrates Autumn ......................................... 51

[19] Middle Path ........................................................... 53

[20] Modern Forgiveness ................................................ 55

[21] My Mother Alone ................................................... 59

[22] Omnibus ................................................................ 63

[23] Open Mind ............................................................ 67

[24] Parallel Lines ......................................................... 69

[25] Poems ................................................................... 73

[26] Potent Boons ......................................................... 74

[27] Prayer ................................................................... 79

[28] Silence .................................................................. 83

[29] Somebody Somewhere ............................................ 84

[30] Tempering ............................................................. 85

[31] Wise Quilt ............................................................. 89

## *[1] Banyan Trees Of Miami*

The Banyan trees of Miami speak to me of mass enlightenment
If something like that is possible...and that is possible I think.
There is no time left today for enlightenment One by One
Avatar by Avatar, Prophet by Prophet
Bodhisattva by Bodhisattva, Christ by Christ.
There is no time left at all.

The Banyan trees of Miami
Spread their meditative canopies over the streets
And deep underground send their strong spiritual roots.
The One God needs to send all of His Prophets,
Buddhas, Avatars down today in a Special Task Force-
And one Banyan tree will not suffice.

What great peace it is to look at the Banyan trees of Miami...

And what great deliverance it will be to behold all His Sons

Meditating beneath their boughs,

And hear sermons of peace and happiness.

## *[2] Being Human*

As I struggle with my prana, my id, my body

The more difficult it became to tame my atma, my ego, my mind.

Oh, my mind is a wild monkey even more intoxicated

By the wines of I and me - this animal looks quite scary, really.

My atma now reaches out to my paramatma, my superego.

I know I needed some intelligence to become spiritual

And learn some physics before I understand metaphysics.

Keeping still, I now focus on developing my mind over matter.

Now tamed, now detoxified, my atma seems to be rising now

To meet the paramatma, my holy spirit.

I see nothing at all - not a dove, not a star, not an angel.

I am just plain human, I guess.

Anyway, I never really understood what they mean

By 'less human' and 'more human'.

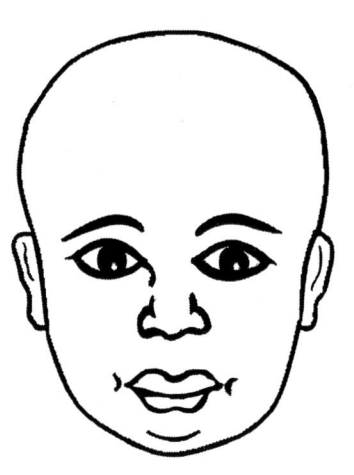

# *[3] Child*

A fresh flower blushing

in her innocent beauty.

A simple star twinkling

in her own radiating light.

A brave butterfly flying

on wings of fancy.

A little lamb

proud in her naivety.

A dazzling diamond

yet to be shaped with skill.

O Child, that's what you are.

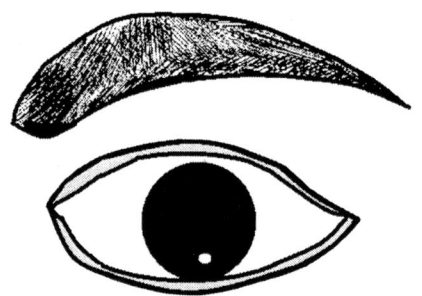

## *[4] Colorful Positives*

There are rewards for being just yourself.

Just a good son, father, husband, brother, friend.

The negatives of life are

Developed well into colorful positives.


Saturn the disciplinarian has

Candidly taught life's lessons.

Jupiter the teacher made me wise,

And still full of wonderment.


I love more people - more people love me.

I have rediscovered myself.

Toxic years went by limping

Because I stood on the firm ground of faith,

Working with my heart.

Lots of heat and smoke

Just made me dark and damp.

There were no heat strokes or skin burns.

Love, patience and prayer healed my wounds.

Sweet karmic fruits with years of ripening

Will provide for the coming years.

## *[5] Donkey Speaks Out*

In the excitement of prodding

The lazy donkey he was riding,

The Master fell off the Donkey's back, and

Broke his own back that

Was stiff with arrogance;

At last the Donkey found his human voice:


O Man, listen!

That Tiger – you call him wild,

But he is more innocent and mild

Than your very own child.


This cute Rabbit – his tail like a cushion,

Was not created for your fashion.

The Buck with his bright eyes, and
The Peacock of multi-dyes,
Are meant only for your eyes.

The Termite so very small,
Is more social than you all.

Ah! this Vulture – he's a scavenger –
He feasts on the flesh of the dead;
But you, your heart n' mind with hatred is fed.

This Locust – labeled as a pest,
Has what you don't – tranquil rest!

Man, these are God's creatures -
They have much better features, and
Much better ethics - than you.
O poor vain Man, think!

The Master's broken back healed,

As he bent with humility, and

Wisdom dawned on him.

# *[6] Effort*

I was walking along the garden path

And saw that the life of effort is pure poetry.

I saw the Lotus in the pond

Making effort to stay far above the muck below.

Pure and blessed, the Lotus bloomed

Making the lonely walker happy.


The Sunflower craned his neck to face the Sun,

And look into his eyes with expectation and courage.

The Sun smiled upon the Flower

Admiring the great risk he was taking.

His petals withered in the burning heat - his colors faded.

Yet his seeds swelled with life-giving oil of knowledge.

The enchanting fragrance of Henna

Makes transient but profound impact.

Crushed into paste on the stone of life

With tears of happiness and sweat of labor

Brings forth the deep red color of wisdom.

The heart is cooled and dyed permanent with Henna

The refreshing fragrance of enlightenment

Still lingers on into the night.

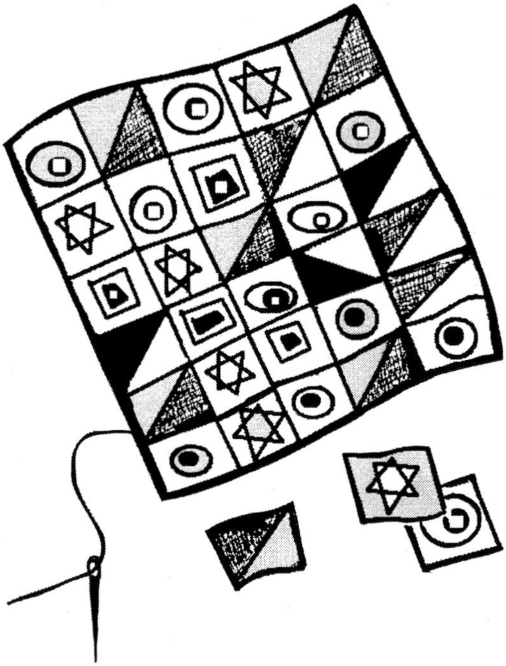

## *[7] Faithful Quilt*

It started as a fine woolen shawl

It felt nice to be softly caressed by its texture.

But as I would wake up

I would find it blown off leaving me cold.

I darned the tears with cotton thread.

Holes patched with muslin, khadi and silk.

Year after year I patched holes and tears with

Fabrics of vivid textures and colors.

Today my shawl is a massive quilt.

Patches of red, green, yellow, blue.

Flowers, spots, checks.

Woven, darned and stitched.

It still feels nice to draw

The heavy sky over my face

And laugh, smile, whisper, weep.

Comforting in winter, suffocating in summer.

Humid in the monsoon,

Moldy and makes me catch a cold.

But I don't mind at all.

Faithfully, it stays on me till I wake up.

## *[8] Futile Feelings*

Chicken wings

Are futile for flying

But great for frying.

The feelings of urban man

Are restricted by doubt

And a stiff upper-lip,

Futile for flying to freedom.

What are the feelings

Of a man in society?

What are the wings

Of the domestic fowl?


Far too well obscured is the heart to read

For those not very close to the heart.

Scores of men have felt well and lost,

For they felt well and did nought.

Hence, must the heart and mind merge.

What are the words n' deeds

Of a man in society?

What are the sturdy legs

Of the champion race horse?

# *[9] Gain and Pain*

More has been said on pain

Than on pleasure.

There is more information on

The pain perception pathway

Than on the pathways of pleasure.

Since excessive pleasure

Peaks out in pain.

Does pain make man more searching

Or maybe - more eloquent?

He further finds the need for

Doctors and mystics,

Gods and shrinks

To hear him and give him

Those wonderful anodynes

To calm his senses.

In his calmness he gains

The absence of pain.

In his calmness he seeks

Pleasure in gainful moderation.

## *[10] I See Good People*

I see good people, very classy people who

Really want to be doing the best

For the folks they love

And for those who are hungry, sick and poor.

They are really kind, good people.


Let's not forget good old IQ, as we talk about EI.

They keep waiting to become rich enough

So they can make a decent donation

Or give a nice gift to Mom,

A gift that's worthy.

And they keep waiting for the best moment.


They waited to collect $100

For the guy sleeping on the street –

He just needed a donut and coffee before

He passed out and away.

They postponed the barbeque

To make it something bigger, a banquet

But the friends left town before

They could become closer.


They postponed sending a money order

To lonely Mom and Dad,

So they could send some respectable amount.

So, old Mom and Dad died waiting.


So mail a card of 25 cents now,

Give Mama a flower today,

And present dear Papa an old hat.

Take the Wife out to the coffee shop

And give her a scarf, never mind the diamond ring.

A dollar a day for the poor guys

On the streets also makes sense.

So the good guy is also a wise guy I think.

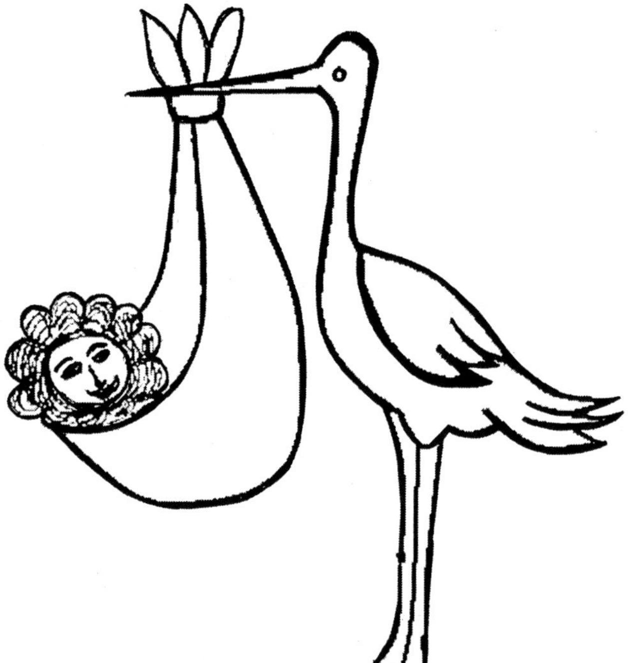

# *[11] Labor*

No one planned this pregnancy

Thirty six weeks ago, yet

Thirty six weeks later

The woman labors to give birth to

A baby that did not ask to be born.

What is the fuss about anyway?

The need to be born is hardly

As great as the need to give birth.

Labor is too painfully exhausting

For a beautiful mystifying birth.

Yet, once born

The need to die is

Almost always as great as

The need to cause death.

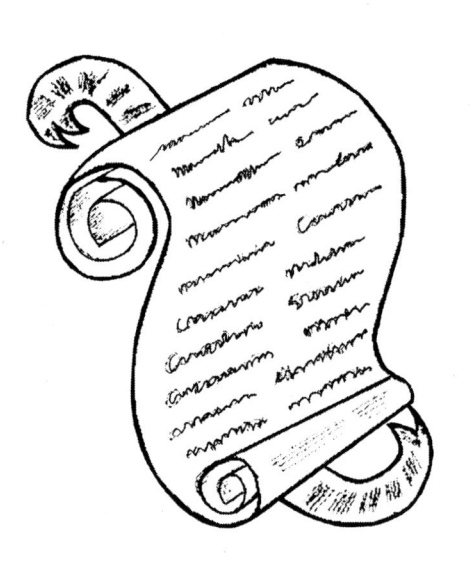

# *[12] Latent Poem*

Created effortlessly, without faltering

Your verses well composed and distinct

Yet merging smoothly, you're my poem of joy.

A poem of hope and inspiration,

Your metaphors handpicked from

The garden of my soul.

Sweet yarns of life solidly

Knit into your fabric,

Soothing my tired mind.

You urge me to win battles

And navigate seas with courage.

So embedded are you in

The depths of my heart that

Ruptures to formalize on paper

Your swelling verses and balmy lyrics.

# *[13] Law Of Gravity*

Coconuts and hope, flowers and happiness -

Many promises of unknown validities,

Ships of alien lands, friendship and courtship

Toss rudderless waiting for kind winds.

Butter of his ego melts on her hot toasted vanity.

Sodium love salts are sprinkled liberally

On greasy sensual steaks,

Both of which increase the risk of heart disease.

Hard to kill habits stimulate growth of habitats.

Marriage made in heaven

Falls through because of the gravity.

Hitting the ground below real hard.

Fortunately there's the law of gravity -

Gravity of a growing family

Saving the foundation of marriage.

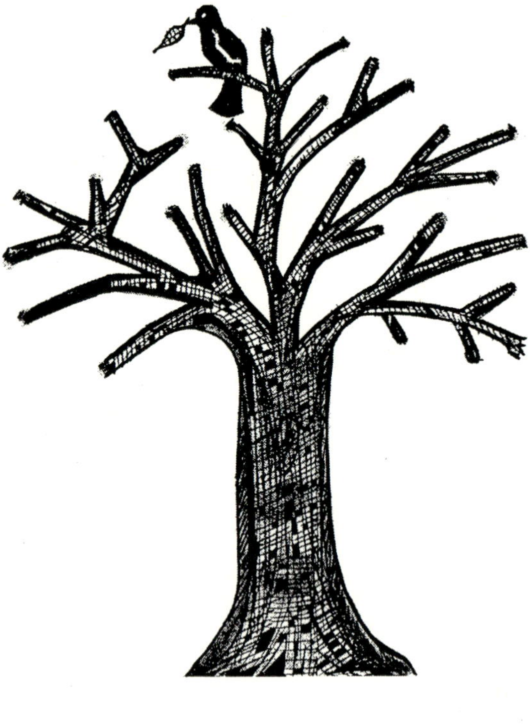

# *[14] Living Alone Is Fun*

Living alone is fun.

I arise with or without the Sun

Eat sour grapes or stale bun,

But the liver has no fun.

(And that is no pun).


Living alone is great.

I write undisturbed on a slate,

My beautiful thoughts of late.

But to read them I have no mate

(And that's not so great).


Living alone is rich.

I walk about my room without a stitch

And sing and dance with a witch,

But when my mind is as black as pitch

No one tells me which is which.

Living alone gives me the kicks.
I can take the best of life's picks
And with anybody I can mix,
But my bills put me in a fix;
O living alone is poor economics!

Living alone makes me feel so high
Whenever I look upwards at the sky
But when I inwardly sigh
For reasons I don't know why,
I know living alone is wry.

That's living alone, my dear men and women,
It's better to live like a hen,
With many others in a pen
Than live alone and read Zen,
To petrify soon – God knows when.
Amen.

# *[15] Magic Land*

Have you heard of the Magic Land, my Father

Of silver waters and golden sands?

Where the Tortoise walks with his held high,

And the Giraffe bends to kiss the Mouse;

Where the Nightingale sings in harmony with the Frog,

And the Dog no more betrays brother Fox.

Have you been to the Magic Land, my Father

Of silver waters and golden sands?

Where God is a man and Men are gods,
And the Servant forgets to rob the Lord;
Where wishes are Horses grazing
On the fertile meadows of illusion,
And every conception of thought
Is superbly delivered in silken ecstasy.

Let us go to this Magic Land, my Father,
And burn the frigidity of the mind.

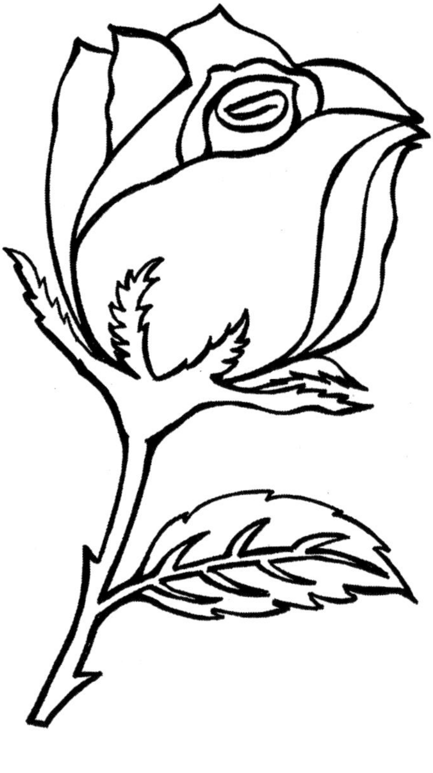

## *[16] Maiden Rose*

Wonderful is this innocent beauty

Of beautiful innocence.

See the lone Rose in the garden -

Where are her friends?

Oh, proudly they went into the wide world,

Hopefully to don a maiden's silken hair

Or her beloved's grave.

They will watch as a friend is broken

Petal by petal by a playful child.

They will watch as their sisters

Wither away at the flower-stalls.

Bees dare not play with these tampered flowers
Sorrowfully they oblige loathsome flies.
But oh! the ecstasy of this lone flower -
Has sorrow seen her face?

The winds gently caress her soft petals,
The bees sing alleluia in her presence,
The birds spread word of her beauty.

She is the Queen, but does she care?

# *[17] Mania*

So I heard when I was a kid:

Help! A mad dog, they cried.

A manic dog had mauled a child –

Kith n' kin of the kid killed the dog,

While the wee human life

Also vanished in the fog.

Two lives had gone

But not the third,

For the dog's kin spared the men,

I heard.

The dog was wrong,

But crazy,

His thoughts were

Much too hazy.

They were no doubt right,

These men,

For they were Men.

# [18] Maple Celebrates Autumn

Unaware of beauty or ugliness

The Maple celebrates autumn's caper

With vivid colors of gold, silver and copper.

Impartial to both prince and pauper

Its riches fall to feed the earth in winter.

In its barrenness, it is the complete survivor.


Oblivious of greatness or humbleness

It stands proud without bending a bough.

The naked tree sieves the heavy snow

The solid water of life, no frills

Let the white stuff fall! it says. No ill will.

Maple sap and syrup will overflow.

Let spring arrive with pomp and show.

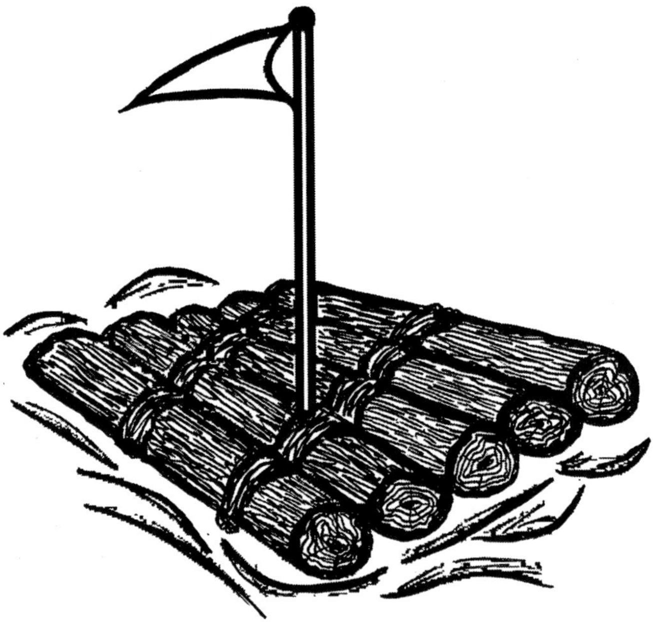

# *[19] Middle Path*

I went jumping from left bank to right,

And right bank to left -

Just to keep afloat

On the turbulent river of life.


I did not teach anybody anything

That they said they did not know.

I am not the Buddha.

Still, at least I understand that

His middle path could be even found

While rafting through the hasty Ganga -

And not only while merrily speeding

Through the super-express highway

Or jogging on the well-designed park lane.


Spiritual saints and saintly spirits of my native land

Protect the righteous and the damned.

I am neither a saint nor a spirit.

Purposefully I kept spiritually sound

For the sake of my family and those I love.

# *[20] Modern Forgiveness*

My mother said, at least pretend

To be happy to see those nasty neighbors;

So then, forgive the politician who speaks like a saint

With the hope that he will really become one;

As an actor who plays the character of Jesus or Rama

In a TV serial may imbibe some sublimity

Despite the lucrative contract.


Hypocrisy is a hesitant step to true goodness

Maybe, just some more effort is required.

Forgive the priest, who had had a sinful history

And forgive the businessman

Who donates millions today despite his greedy past.


Forgive the chemical industry that is going green now,

Forget its deadly errors of omissions

And global horror of emissions;

Yes, sin should not be in the first place,

Nor the corporation be corrupt,

It is as the first temptation or the betrayal at the last supper.

Yet the divine forgive these trespasses

With the faith that the children will inherit

Fresh air, loving hearts, clean minds and green environments,

And with the hope that the doves of peace

Do not drop dead due to global warming or die by crashing into

Deceptive glass scaffolding of glittering skyscrapers.

# *[21] My Mother Alone*

Mother, my Mother, my Mother alone
so I perceived when the sun first shone
for me.

Only she could offer that affection
none other could or would give substitution
for me.

Mother, my Mother, my Mother alone
silently hardships she had borne
for me.

Could I have repaid her well, fully well
even with a lifetime penance in a well
for me?

I might as well ask the Creator

this - who only than her is greater

for me.

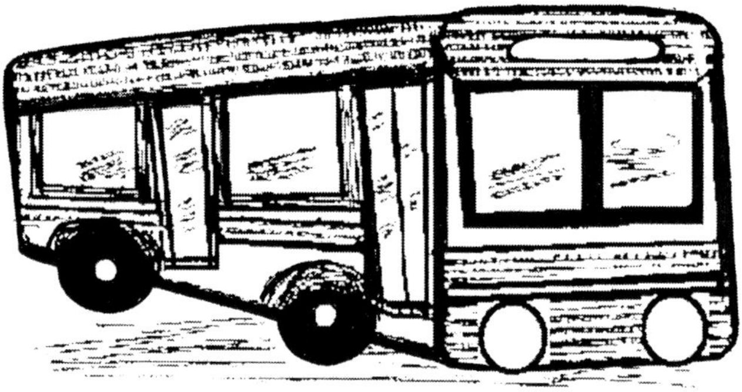

# *[22] Omnibus*

The metromonk on this bus is enchanted

By unique multicultural faces before him.

He stares without being rude at people

Whose expectations in getting respect

Far exceed their abilities for compassion.


Creased faces from troubled nations

Now incredulously peaceful and happy.

No one follows them dangerously close.

Pampered teenagers loudly chatter.


One mature voice pierces through their shrieks.

Someone talks to himself. All listen.

But he is speaking to no one.

He enjoys his right of speech--

A right denied in lands of collective insanity.

This omnibus is blessed by the Omniscient.
Man is a stranger on his own planet, yet
This bus opens its doors to Man's divine nature.

The Omnipotent trusts that Man will find
Meaning in traveling in peace with his brothers
Without forsaking his unique seat in life.

The wandering monk wonders
If he could stop from time to time at
The inns of life despite his adventures.

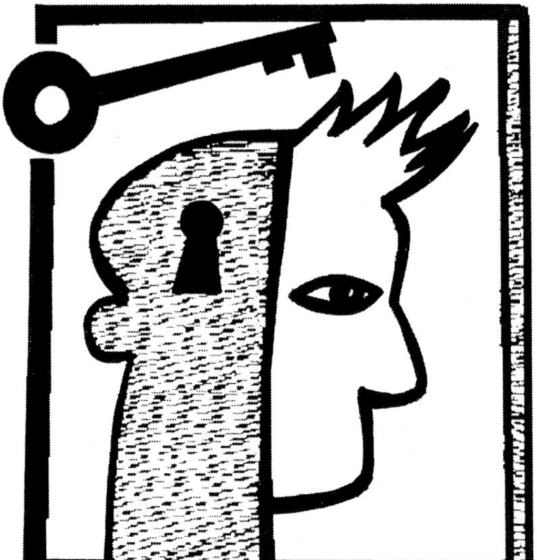

# *[23] Open Mind*

Open your mind for friendship,

Open your mind to love.

Mind the windows of your mind

With bolts of courage and wisdom

To withstand friendship attacking

Your open mind with motives

And love stripping it of sanity.

Open your mind for learning,

Open your mind to progress.

Mind you that your open mind

Is at the most a recycle bin

Not a trashcan of foul stuff

Meant for the incinerator.

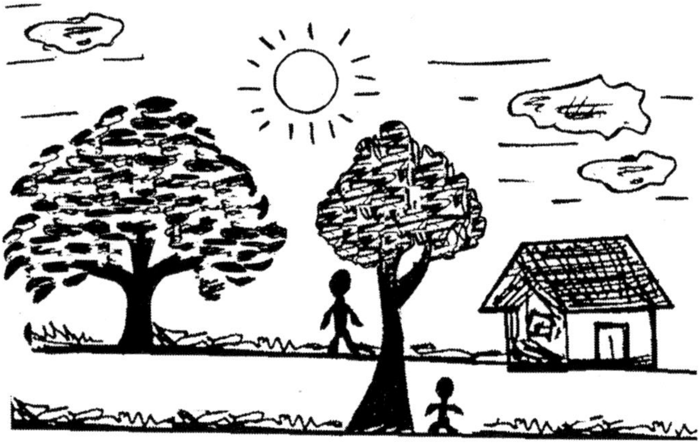

## *[24] Parallel Lines*

We walk in parallel lines.

When did they begin,

where will they end?

Afraid to stop, to meet.

So we go on and on.

Never stopping - never meeting.

We hesitate to walk in line

too proud to follow the other.

Strange journey, stranger ways,

unknown destinations.

In the beginning probably

our spirits burnt incense.

These tired lines will certainly

end where our parallel biers

burn into paranormal ashes.

The geometry is killing me.

Can we rest together

at the inns of life

from time to time

and place to place?

# *[25] Poems*

Fleeting ideas

Captured in nets of reason.

Patches of paint

Brushed into believable scenes.

Dirt from the riverbed

Molded into models

And fired by imagination.

Ravings of a fevered brain

Recorded on tape.

Borderline psychosis

Finding its own therapy.

Understanding enters

As consciousness exits.

# [26] Potent Boons

The devotee begged of Lord Ganesha:
Lord help me overcome the barriers to communication
And make me in your likeness.

Said the Lord to the faithful mortal:
What will you do with my dysmorphic features
In your world of perceived perfection?

Answered the privileged beggar:
Give me a big head with large storage capacity
And faster access to information;
Make my eyes narrow for meditation
And protect me from distraction.

# [25] Poems

Fleeting ideas

Captured in nets of reason.

Patches of paint

Brushed into believable scenes.

Dirt from the riverbed

Molded into models

And fired by imagination.

Ravings of a fevered brain

Recorded on tape.

Borderline psychosis

Finding its own therapy.

Understanding enters

As consciousness exits.

# *[26] Potent Boons*

The devotee begged of Lord Ganesha:

Lord help me overcome the barriers to communication

And make me in your likeness.

Said the Lord to the faithful mortal:

What will you do with my dysmorphic features

In your world of perceived perfection?

Answered the privileged beggar:

Give me a big head with large storage capacity

And faster access to information;

Make my eyes narrow for meditation

And protect me from distraction.

Grant me large ears to listen well

With the memory of an elephant;

And long probing nose for curiosity

And feedback from the environment.


Hide my big mouth so that

I speak rightly only when required;

And provide me with single small tusk

For the just needed assertiveness.


Give me a good tummy to eat well

And be happy and contented;

Above all, I pray for the boon of

Humility to befriend the smallest mouse

Who may care to listen to me.

Said the Lord of Communicators

To the prostrated creature:

I'll grant you all that you ask for –

But in spite of these potent boons

Should you be afflicted by the deadly syndrome

With symptoms ranging from

Conceptual constipation and verbal diarrhea

Then only Father,

The almighty Mahadeva can save you.

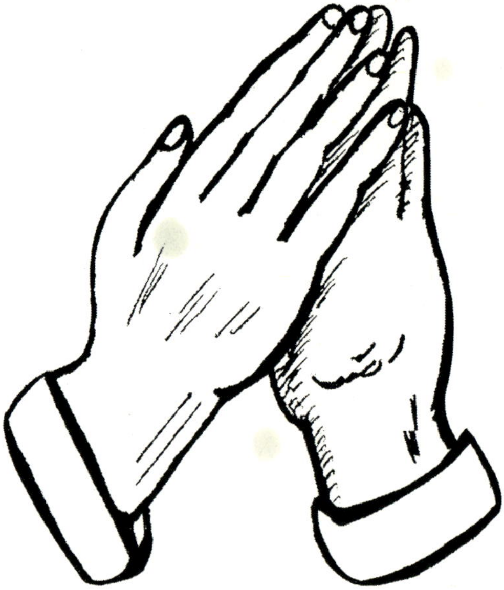

## *[27] Prayer*

Usually, the Sage prayed for others selflessly.

Today, he prayed selfishly:

You have made my senses sharp -

Help me polish them daily

On the grindstone of wisdom.

My senses work overtime -

In the process develop my sixth.

My sturdy legs carry me through

The gutters of human decadence

Do not let them tarry –

Delay not till I am too old

For earthly indulgences.

' and straight.

loveless, and

ness to the unforgiving.

My desires are many –

Harness me gently.

Make me feel even before I think.

Your prizes for my shams

I will shamefully return.

I dare not judge others,

For you have unconditionally

Given me love.

Judge me now, when I am

Neither old nor confused

Nor too dull to understand your justice.

Wait not till I age and repent

Over my energy spent.

Judge me now, so that I can

Accept life as

A precious gift from Life.

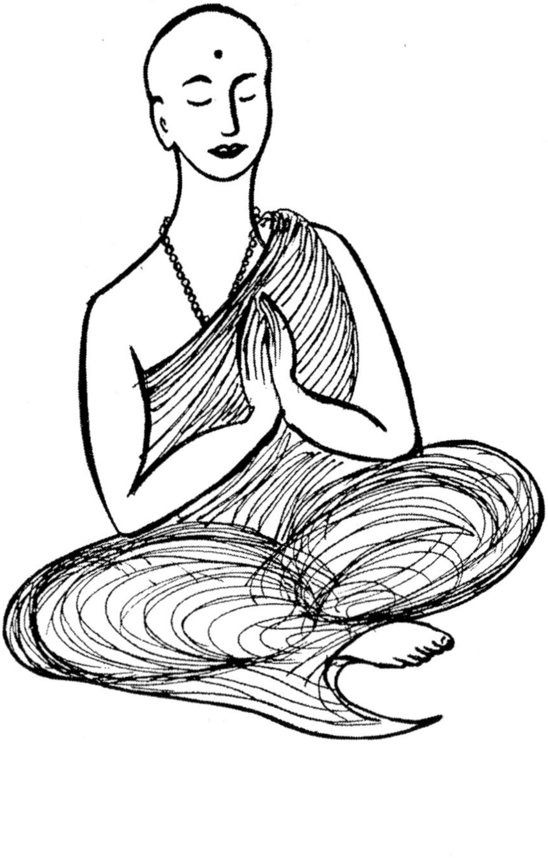

# *[28] Silence*

When ideas fail let us read good poetry.

When conversation fails let us read silence.

There is hope in the pregnancy of silence.

The hope of feminine virtues

And robust virile dogmas.

The hope of fertile ideas

And a sacred fruit.

The hope of a holy communion.

The hope of hearing better things

And saying things well.

# [29] *Somebody Somewhere*

The believer approached the Wise Man

For his blessings.

His blessings came with a price – said he:

Go my friend, go -

Somebody somewhere needs your help.


He's suffering a hell of violence,

Burning in the furnace of anger, and

Groping in the darkness of ignorance.

He is agonized in his immense luxury,

Drowning in his private pool of ego, and

Is sorrowing in his brother's joy.


Go my friend, go quickly –

Go in haste, lest he destroy himself.

# *[30] Tempering*

Said the Sage

To the woman in white:

A volcanic explosion dared threaten

Peace in your home.

Your soul survived the blaze

As it drew energy from the very fire

That came to destroy.

Your natural wisdom set by lava

Became the rock on which

The temple of your family's faith is built.

You patiently waited for the calm

Because what started must end.

So that others can rejoice

You rejoiced in being alive –

With an innocence

That unnerved the fiery monster.


You do not need any more teaching,

You are enlightened.

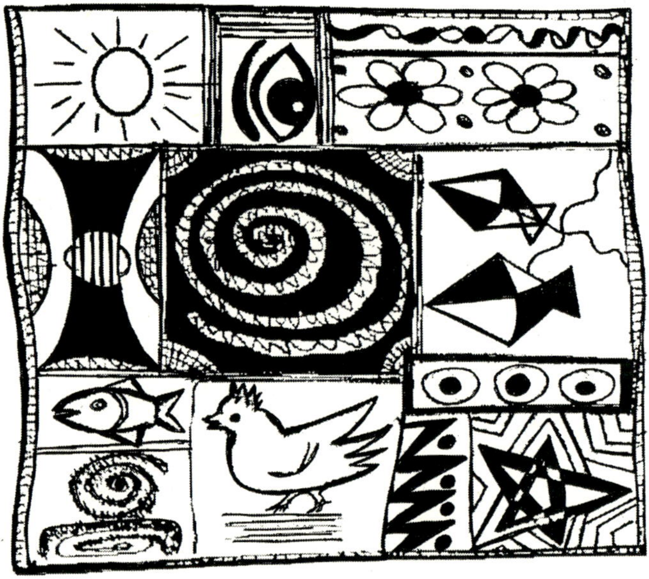

# *[31] Wise Quilt*

My strange patched and darned quilt

Is still warm on me.

Can't be replaced by my fine blankets

Lying in prosperous closets.

For once upon a time it was my shawl

And I took the trouble of

Turning it into a quilt.

People praise my layered quilt.

They say how fine and thick it is.

How I would be cold without it.

Such harmonious patterns

I have made with beautiful cloths.

I love my quilt.

And see in its diverse fabrics -

My story spread out in collage.

I've so much to do before I snuggle under it.

But at least I taught a silly shawl the way -

How to be my wise quilt.